# Artemas & Ark:

## the Ridge and Valley poems

*poems by*

# Jerry Wemple

*Finishing Line Press*
Georgetown, Kentucky

# Artemas & Ark:

## the Ridge and Valley poems

Publisher: Leah Maines

Editor: Christen Kincaid

Cover Art: *Then* painting by Lisa M. Budd

Author Photo: Jerry Wemple

Cover Design: Elizabeth Maines McCleavy


Order online: www.finishinglinepress.com
           also available on amazon.com

Author inquiries and mail orders:
Finishing Line Press
P. O. Box 1626
Georgetown, Kentucky 40324
U. S. A.

# Table of Contents

Epilogue

*There is a prophet within us, forever whispering that behind the seen lies the immeasurable unseen.*

—Frederick Douglass

*Yahweh said to Satan, "Where have you come from?" Then Satan answered Yahweh and said, "From going back and forth on the earth, and from walking up and down on it"*

—Book of Job, 1:7 (REV)

# Prologue:
# Sunbury, Pa., 1957

There is an uncertainty that grips us
like the gray water grips the last few

chunks of river ice in these last few
minutes of light on a day in the ending

weeks of winter, a winter that was
not much of a winter. You hope that

spring might become something more
of a season. Whatever good hope might do.

On this graveled shore, the Front Street
traffic noise fades in and out. Long

lines of water run to oblivion.
There is illusion, and what remains.

Here the river joins it branches—
north and west—and funnels its way south.

Between Sunbury and Blue Hill are ghosts:
the old toll bridge, remembered only by those

who themselves are near apparitions.
The black iron train bridge—once

the world's sharpest turn for a rail
line. Gone, but when?

The white bridge, built after the floods,
the kids no longer call it new.

Gray wall, foot thick, ten, fifteen, twenty feet
high. Built to hold back flood waters.

What does it hold in? The sun slips
behind the rock outcrop of the hill.

Gray becomes grayer then evaporates.
The water's edge is indistinct.

# Book I:
# Artemas

# Happy as the day

Happy as the day is long, Artemas
begins his stroll each a.m., *a' nine 'xact*,
he claims when asked, though few do. Who would?
Those about know wastrels and his stale show.

Artemas is the finest fellow in all
downtown. He knows all the old, long-gone stores,
and where each brick used to be. Keeps a token
from the defunct bridge ready in his pocket.

A broken bird in flight, a stain against
the gray sky, that's what Artemas sure seems.
Now fallen from his perch, he walks 'til woods
thicken. Notices fences even here. *Why?* asks he.

# Artemas cries

Artemas cries like a babe deprived
of his fooler, or the real thing. *Paah,*
he says. The wise owl ignores him. Not even
a *Who* are you? Snubbed once more, he thinks.
Yet, yet, an idle stray wanders by, casts in with

Artemas' lot. Rheumy-eyed, threadbare
as stuffed dolls found in the musty attic
of an abandoned house, they lock in
together, march on in the morn. *It's new
now,* Artemas exclaims. Believes it too.

# Moontown I

The washwoman's bucket suds the alley.
Spent soap sifts through Artemas' feet. Soaked.
*Madam, I'm Adam.* He doffs his top. Dog
bows. *You're not the first fellow to use that*

*line*, says she. Spins and shifts to hanging clothes.
*Don't be rough*, says the newborn man.
*I extend a hand.*          *Best sit there on that stoop,*
says she. *Hang your socks on the rail. A mug*

*of soup for you, a water dish for dog.*
*Maid's day off*, she laughs, because she is
a maid, down at the hotel. Artemas thanks
for the kindness. Dog rests head on her feet.

## Moontown II

Afternoon skims into evening. *'Spect you want
a supper*, says she.     *Haint done a thing for
it yet*, says he. Artemas grabs a broom,
sweeps the walk. And again. Hoses garden

Tomatoes out back. Chicken leg and beans,
green, on the porch. Meat off the bone for dog.
Artemas wanders to a field edge, there
sleeps off supper. The woman pressed an old

Coat upon him. *Back for breakfast*, she bid.
In the a.m., he presents. *Handy with
a hammer. Done dug with shovel*, says he,
between bites of biscuit. So begins.

# Moontown III

Joke's on him: her name is Eve. *Blessed be,*
says he. *Wasn't being smart. You near sharp*

*enough*, says she. Pact made. One becomes three.
Three become one. Dog sleeps in a peaceful

kingdom. Sun shines in glory summer. Night
moves Artemas from field to house. A new

start. A new man. Artemas spends mornings
working at the house, afternoons in odd

jobs around town. Evenings back with Eve.
Tales abound about how it all began.

*You're an original*, claims Eve. *So
they say,* says Artemas. Dog whispers sleep.

# Artemas labors in the field

Hope fell down with rain, drenching soil, soaking
the world and its roots. *Let it rain*, Artemas
said. He felt it wash the sweat from him, felt
it cleanse him. Artemas remembers long

ago, when he was but a boy on errand:
a man stealing bread in the grocery,
a man in a dirty coat and spent boots,
and the shame the boy Artemas saw, sad

shame. Artemas knows that like Adam he
must always labor for his feast. *Reward
will come*, says he, *if not in this world then*

*perhaps the next.* Sun slinks back. Artemas
puts hoe to ground. *No shame in that*, says he,
*None 'tall.* The bright sun shifts into dusky sky.

# Artemas on Good Friday

Artemas goes to the old church, the one
a bit nearer, but where the priest is deaf
and oft wanders away from the lectern
during homilies leaving a sprinkling
of grayed parishioners to question
if they will receive the host. But today

the priest has passion. Points to the stations
of the cross encircling the sanctuary.
*Jesus fell*, he says. *This man helped*, he
proclaims. Artemas understands. He beats
his breast as the acolyte rings treble bells
thrice. The high sound floats, then settles in the room.

# Artemas on Maundy Thursday

After supper, Artemas goes walking
past the streets down to the river. Dips his
hands into the murky water, brings rain
over his scarred brow. A lone crow swoops and
startles Artemas. He turns and trudges
toward the hill. Once there Artemas sits
on a park bench near the pavilion, smells
the new spring flowers, smoke from kids across
the way, there in the shadow just outside
the lamplight. Artemas stares west. The lights
of the town flicker in the haze. A moon
glow makes the river a flowing ribbon.
A bell tolls the hour. *Praise Jesus,* says he.

# Artemas goes to school

On his way, Artemas picks a posy:
simple flower, simple man—Daisy. Her name too.
School's all in. Children at desks, desks in rows.
Boys with white shirts and ties; girls with skirts or
jumpers. Artemas approves the scene. He's
from the old school. Artemas is beguiled,
a middling man found love. The teacher his new
wife. Tap-tap on the window, hands daisy
through an open pane. Teacher shushes him
away while girl children giggle. *Spring has come,*
says he. The sun darts in and out of clouds,
but who cares, he thinks. Let it rain.

## Artemas kills his woman

A terrible blow. *Then came a departure.*
*Thereafter nothing fell out as it might or*
*ought.* Twisted metal and frail consequence.
Artemas first remembers nothing.
Then all. Smells of rubber and gasoline.
Metallic taste of blood. Feel of wrenched bones.
Worse: the sound of no sound. No reply. No, no,
Artemas thinks. The drive: a simple country
mile? A picnic? A visit? He knows not.
It is an image he never shares that
keeps him silent for days, weeks, months. It is
inevitable that he is abandoned.

## Between Hell and Hell

                    and he felt so bad when he saw the traces
                    of old lies still on their faces

For ninety-one days Artemas lay prone.
He awoke to a cruel trick. It was
all over. Ashes. Dust. Memory. His thoughts
scrambled on a tricked tongue to strangers. Words now
puzzles. What is a tree? What is car?
Who is death? I hate to tell you what they
tried. At least they tried. But beer, and whiskey,
smokes, and long talks on the porch seemed no
use. Seemed to them. But scrambled Artemas
knew. He saw. He felt. He was. He is.

## Days and months go

Days and months go. Artemas keeps his own
time. Some say they saw him day before last
buying a paper out of the rack in
front of Henry's Market. Time before, he
was talking with a carnie on game row
at the fair. Past summer neighbor Joe spoke
to Artemas about keeping his lawn cut.
Next day, Joe's lawn was freshly mowed. Hedges
trimmed nice, too. Joe ended up cutting
Artemas' yard. *Simpler that way*, Joe said.
For now Artemas is a simple man, who
bends time and space like a fantastic machine.

## There Stands the Glass

Artemas lifts his first of the day, does
not think about his next nor next. They will
come after a walk into town, toast and
coffee at Dot's Diner, just a bit past

when the clerks and secretaries have left
for their stores and offices. Some days he rises
early, makes Mass at Saint Michael's, smiles at
the Sisters and their children gathered

there in the darkened sanctuary.
To the right of the priest on the altar
is a statue of the Virgin. Her bare
feet crush the gray-green serpent beneath her.

## Most days

Most days, Artemas makes his rounds: the Chestnut
Street Inn opens in the forenoon. Edgar's is
out of the way, not much of a lunch crowd.
In the warm months, he'll sit in the park,
watch the kids leave school at three, trickle down
the sidewalk sparkling like cut glass. They know
not to mock him; once one tried and was
chastised for it. It was a Bridy kid. An
older cousin cuffed and cursed him. He does
no harm, they say. Mostly he's ignored.
Artemas rises to make Tony's at four.

# The Derivation of Artemas

I am a Jew, set to trade and tinker
in these brown hills, these green valleys. Perhaps
an Igbo man, wild-haired and sweating, moving
fast through creek beds and summer nights. A bohunk
tromping to the Shendo mine before first
light. A German farmer who has no use
for town, though my favorite daughter lives
in a city and my boy spends Saturdays
in a beer garden. I am among the last
Susquehannock, massacred by the Paxton
Boys in Lancaster December. I am
a man in the woods on the hill. I am
a man at the edge of the river. I am.

## A Daemon Called Love

Here's the trick: Daisy grew in shade. Fair
flower, unfair. It was the young priest—Laughlin—
courted her in shadows. Then trouble left town.

Daisy kept her secret as it grew. Then lost it.
Alone now, she pressed on: Kept her charges
at the Sisters' school, made confession at

some distant parish, returned the smile
of Artemas on the second Sunday
of Ordinary Time. Guileless

Artemas is flattered by the fair
flower, never ponders sudden charms and
affections. He supposes himself a catch.

Though a woodsman's son, he dresses now in
store-bought suits, has a counselor's shingle.
And fair is fair when you try, Daisy has

convinced herself. And so Artemas turns
from suitor to spouse. Though Daisy's heart
is not in it, she holds his steady hand.

Things go well enough. Yet troubled smudged is
not trouble smote. One night, Laughlin returned with
no change of heart, only a change of his clothes.

.

# Quietus

There are those who say they knew all along, those
who say they had their suspects. There are those
who called him friend, but betrayed him
with a lack of a whisper, a word. Still
a moon-blind man is hard to reckon. They
kept their own counsel till it was too far,
too much. Much too much for simple Artemas.

None claimed to see it, but Big Anders
the fireman was upon it first. Pointed
out the lack of skid marks, the car just off
center of the tree, still running when he
got there. Artemas, alone and bloodied,
mumbling the names of Daisy and the young
priest and a bit Anders couldn't quite cipher.

# A damn shame

*A damn shame*, Artemas says, and spits into
the river. Gray water sullies south. He
groans. Knees weak and crackling like thin, dry
branches, Artemas climbs the steep bank. *I'm worn*
he says aloud, though no one is near.
The sun sets at his back. He heads to town.
A few coins jingle in his pocket. He stops
at the hot dog place, asks Sam to pour
a coffee to go. *'ank you, fer everythin'*,
Artemas says. At first Sam thinks it queer,
then nods an understanding. Artemas goes.
He limps along the lead-colored sidewalk,
pointing toward home. The sky darkens and
the air cools. *Won't be long*, Artemas sure
thinks. Just cannot be. A night storm approaches.

# Repose

Artemas's heart grows wide like the river.
It is calm like a spring pond. *It is time,*
he tells the woman. *It 'ime.* She nods
brings another damp cloth. He inches his
leaden head and chest above the narrow
bed. *Got lon' walkin' ahead,* says he. *No'*
*sure what's up there.    Rest now,* says she, knowing
fully well the rest is just beginning.
Artemas blurs, closes his eyes, opens them,
gazes at the room's blue walls. The color flows
like liquid. Artemas rises until he
melds into the evening and forever.

# Artemas lives

Artemas lives in the hearts of all of us who have come down from the gray-green wooded hills to the valley of the green-gray river which flows to the salted sea. *In nomine patris et filii et spiritus sancti.* These dusted words float over Artemas as the river carries him, as it does us all, to the salted sea. Bless him. Bless us, all. In the end as it was in the beginning: it is a long, lonely river only made less so if we dare bear the intricate weight of companionship. It is a mixt and profound river, and we and he simple beings doing as best we can with what we've been presented.

# A Song for Artemas

Trapped like the angels of heaven, we
endure, sad and sullen. Huddled around

empty boxes, fearful of those who left,
and those who remain. We offer no sound,

no remorse, nothing at all. Exiting now
is one who will not return. Though a few

sometimes do. We pity them most. Bless them all.
Their eyes watchful on us: God shelters fools.

Haze of an April evening fog settles
over the river, then the town. A bell rings

from the stone church, echoed by another
blocks distant. A kind of song, a needful thing.

# Interlude:
# Years later

## Years later

Years later, a boy (though nearly a man),
rubs a brass bit in his pocket; it's not

a coin, more a just token of long past
days. He walks the empty alleys, his feet

clomping echoes off cracked brick and cinder
block back walls of the Market Street stores:

most long gone, all but escaped from memory.
Smells of the Chinese restaurant mix

with garbage and faint industrial odor:
oiled boards and rusted steel drums,

piss-poison chemicals leaching. Timmy Shaffer, on
break from the pizza shop, leans against its

screen door, smoking, nods hello to the boy
as he shuffles on, making steady progress.

The boy gazes toward the darkening sky:
*Gonna be a hell of a moon tonight,*

says he, as he slides into the streetlamp light.
A wind rises from the south, bringing warmth.

# Book II:
# Ark

# Rain: Ark Defeats Triumph

He understands. The weight of the machine
slips away. Ark anticipates the dull thud
of the bike on the wide oak ten yards down.
But tires catch on a dry patch. The bike rights.
Ark's left foot gears down and he goes slowly
home. Months later he's running the bike
up and down Chestnut Street, going with
the traffic, then against. Except there's
not much traffic since it's three a.m.
The bike drifts past the closed stores, the bar
on the corner of Second Street, funeral
home a couple more blocks down, machine and its
rider like ghosts, hardly noticed over
the rumblings of the long-haul trailer trucks
coming off the state hill onto Front Street.
Still, Ark knows the cops are coming so he
heads down the alley and cuts the motor.
Pushes the heavy machine out back of
Fat Barnacle's place, past Furman's garage.

# A Tangled Web

Daisy and Laughlin made an unfaithful
escape. They were still unsettled when she
made her confession. She would have a child.
The priest knew how to count. It would not be
his; he bade her return to Artemas,
but Daisy knew there was no Artemas
to return to, or at least not the same
man he once was. And he thinks her dead now.
She's dead to him. The priest, as was his habit,
left again. And Daisy had the little
bastard, though technically that's not right. Still
she scorned him. For a while they moved from
hovel to hovel, then settled in a little
block house in the lower end of town. At school
no one much cared. Everyone else had their own
complaints against an indifferent world.
At recess, the boy sat in a corner
of the yard whilst the sun shone upon him.

# A Flower Rests

Daisy rose later in the morning each
day until she barely rose at all. Ark
was left to get his own breakfast: peanut
butter smeared on doughy bread, a pale
apple in a paper bag to take for school
lunch. He would shuffle down the slate sidewalks
parallel to the river street doing his
best to slow time and the inevitable.
After school, the return trip home and sometimes
there deposited on the couch in front of
a blurred television his mother
like a monument to a forgotten
whatever. Sometimes she would cook supper and
sometimes not. And sometimes the old neighbor
woman would stop by to say *mind if I
borra ya boy for a while* and then sit
him at her kitchen table and stuff him full
on potatoes and greasy hamburger
and sometimes apple pie that was not too bad.

# Night

Night falls suddenly when the sun declines
behind these rolling hills. The boy sits on
the river side of the flood wall, his back
to the town. He smokes a cigarette, counts
the cars and tractor trucks on the state road
across the water. Wonders where they're bound.
The boy would like a car, some way, any way
to leave the town, to drive past the farms
until the hills grow and the woods thicken
and sit beside the tiny stream that is the start
of this half-mile wide river. The boy rises,
heads into town. He walks past the little park,
a few blocks up Market, enters a tiny hot
dog restaurant, nods to Old Sam, who started
the place after the war. Sam knows, fixes
one with everything, uncaps a blue birch
from the old dinged metal floor cooler,
while the boy fingers the token in
his pocket. Outside the wind rises and shifts.

# A Good Day

There on the edge of memory, Ark sees
the man who wandered around town. Ark

searches back to when he was only five, when
Ark would wander alleys hunting for bottles

to return to the store for nickels and dimes.
Sometimes he'd search the old rail yard, looking

for a heavy spike or other treasure.
Once he found a dollar there. And once he

saw the man, sitting near the top of the steps
of the yardmaster's tower. Ark wandered

up to him. *Can see lots from here*, the man
said. He pointed at a vague distance. *There*

*was th' toll bridge. Gone. New one ain't nice. Plain.*
The man looked down and looked away again.

Ark studied the man as he stared at
the slant of the rooftops, at the glint

off the river just beyond. You have this,
the man said, and handed him a dulled brass

token. *No good anymore. Maybe one day*
*might be.* Ark sat on the rusty step next

to the man puzzling over the token
and the man, but he was far too young to

cipher their meaning. Still, Ark enjoyed
the gift, which seemed a treasure. The pair sat

in silence a good while longer, until
the noon whistle sounded, echoing through the town.

Then Ark rose, put the token in his jeans
pocket, walked down the steps and looked back

once before heading down the alley. He
waved as the man cried out: *Good day, goo da.*

# Rituals

The man from that day and a woman came
often to morning Mass. Ark remembers them

from the years he went to the Sisters' school.
The man and the woman sat quietly

in the back. The children sat quietly,
assembled by grade, in the wooden pews

at the front of the sanctuary. Ark
would stare straight ahead at the polished stone

of the altar, the bronze chalice, the crown
of thorns and the crimson drops speckling

the solemn figure on the crucifix.
On Sundays Ark walked alone to church,

sat in the back, on the side, unnoted.
Some Sundays, the couple would wait

for Ark in the vestibule near the bright
silver holy water tank by the statue

of Saint Joseph. The woman would press
a dollar into Ark's hand, say he was good,

handsome, smart. The man did not often speak.
Mostly he would nod, look away, nod

again. Ark always said thank you as he stood
there, eyes down, puzzled by the ceremony

while he fingered the bit of brass in his
pocket remembering how it came to him.

## Ark at Thirteen

Chipped brick sidewalks make bike wheels rumble.
Ark stops at the bat-battered stop sign. Rests

his feet on the ground. He stares down
Church Street alley, toward the river and

the mountain beyond it, the sky filling
with early evening color. Soon the sun

will slip behind the hills. He's got no place
to go. His mother, no longer cares, if

she ever, offers no regard. Ark roams
feral. Pats his pocket for cigarettes,

feels the Marlboro box, removes it, counts
the smokes: four left. He fishes a lighter

from deep in his pocket. Lights one. *Three now,*
he thinks as he watches the ember glow.

# Just then, a distant hum

Just then, a distant hum grows closer,
clearer. The black and white barricade arm

draws down. Bells clip a stunted staccato song.
Blocks distant, the horn sounds steady, low, loud.

And then the rumble is near, and passing. Ark
draws on his cigarette. Counts boxcars with

names of distant places. Boxcars headed to
distant places: Harrisburg, Baltimore. *Who*

*knows*? Ark wonders. Ark waves to a man on
the caboose platform. The man, dressed in coveralls,

stares blank-face straight past Ark. The railroader
flicks the remains of a mostly smoked

stogie, hot ash and all hitting Ark square
in the chest. Ark looks up to glimpse a small

trail of golden tobacco juice leaking from
a corner of the railroad man's crooked mouth.

# Ark and the girl were

Ark and the girl were in love. Her name could
have been Cynthia or Jane, Lisa, Debra,

or Susan. But it was not. It was Lilith:
a name her mother got from a magazine,

a fanciful name for a plain place. Still,
it suited her, a bit whimsical, full

of promise. They'd known each other since
about forever. On a summer playground

he watched her skip rope and they moved
on schoolyard swings together. A couple years

later, Ark sometimes walked her home from school
though he lived on the far side of town. They

were young then, and that was all there was right
then. One summer the girl moved, not far, but

to a nice house on a hill in a tract
outside town. That was all there was, for then.

# Resurrection/Inheritance

Winter gives way to late winter gives way
to early spring. The seasons drag on the way

they do. Ark outgrew the Sisters' school, entered
the town high school one fall. By Lent that next

year, Ark noticed that the man and woman
had not come to Sunday church in a long

while, though he could not remember just when
they stopped. On Easter Sunday, Ark went

to the earliest of three masses, knowing
it would be less crowded. He saw the woman

there, she slipped in just ahead of him,
quiet as a ghost. This time it was he

who waited for her in the vestibule,
fully knowing she had something to say.

*He's gone*, she said at first, and paused. *You
remember years ago when he gave you*

*a coin of sorts, a token? You were kinda
small then. He wanted you to have this too,*

she said, and handed Ark an envelope
like an offertory. Ark understood

now, in a moment of intuitive
and inexplicable clarity, that this

was his inheritance. In the envelope
was a rubber-band bounded raft of bills

most small denominations, most torn or
wrinkled: a poor man's treasure. Stumbling some,

Ark gave his condolence, thanked her best
he could. Something unspoken between them

let the other know they knew what it was
all about. Outside, Ark tucked the packet

deep in his pocket, zipped his jacket
against the wind and morning chill. Ark walked

Market Street a while, then the alleys home,
moving slowly to keep his heart down. Even

though it was Easter, when he got to Furman's
garage, he let himself in the yard gate,

walked up to the back door of the house,
and knocked. Ark heard some television noise

and some commotion coming from the front
room. One of the mop-headed grandkids let

him in the kitchen and then Furman came
out, puzzled by the timing of the visit.

Ark was all business. *How much you
take for that Triumph motorcycle*? he asked.

# Triumph

Ark tinkered with the machine for a day
or so, wanted all to be perfect. He

knew there was no need. Furman was a top
mechanic, especially when it came

to English imports: BSA, Norton,
Triumph. Furman wondered where Ark got

the money, but didn't ask. He had learned
that most times it's best that a person's

business is his business. Besides, Ark
never caused that kind of trouble, none at all

that Furman could remember. He had known
Ark since he was a little kid fetching

his mother cigarettes and soda from
the corner grocery. Sometimes Ark would

stop by the garage, standing quietly on
the edge, watching him work. Sometimes Furman

would give Ark small jobs: cleaning spark plugs,
rehanging tools on the peg board. The past

few summers Ark rode along with Furman
to auctions in the next county over where

he'd buy beaters for parts, newer ones for
selling. Though Ark would answer when asked,

and would sometimes ask his own questions, he
was often silent as stone during those

rides. He just has a worried mind, Furman
figured. Guessed he would too if he was him.

# Farmer

Every time I plant a seed
He said kill it before it grow

Sometimes she called him Farmer, not often,
just now and then. It was a curious

thing since he lived in town, with only a little
grass patch out back of his house, cracked concrete

out front. Ark was not like the real country
kids, classmates who drove jacked-up pickups

into town on Friday and Saturday
nights, riding the Market Street circuit,

blaring metal and country, killing time,
wasting gas. Once and a while a few of them

might pull over near the Legion, sit on
the cement bench smoking, talk about finding

somebody's older cousin to buy beer
or a pint. Ark avoided that scene, kept

to the alleys, the edges of town, though sometimes
on warmer nights he'd climb the black metal fire

escape steps of the old City Hotel, now
empty and derelict, sit at the edge

of the roof watching the parade. From ten
stories up he could see most of the town:

the lights of the stores and bars, the river
to the west, big rigs on the other side

heading north and south along the state road.
Sometimes, up there, Ark pulled the girl's picture

from his wallet, conjured them sharing this
quiet world for a brief and peaceful moment.

She called him Farmer and he did
not question why. He accepted and let

her grow in his heart. It was simply one
of the funny things he liked about her.

# The Yardmaster's Tower

Ark flies into the night, going farther
each time. Darkness seeks to envelop him
as he casts off fiery sparks burning
into a velvet sky. He wakes in sweat,

the darkness of his room, returns slowly
to its dullness. Still an hour from first light,
Ark dresses in jeans and a ragged flannel
shirt, boots. His feet tap a slow rhythm in

the brick alley, up steel steps. One flight, then two.
He sits on a rusty deck, looks over the old
rail yard. A memory rises: nearly as gone
as this place itself, now lit in pink-orange.

He pulls a worn token from his pocket,
considers it a moment, then rises and
walks steadily into the full golden
chill of morning, happy for the day.

# Though he did not know

Though he did not know him, just knew of him,
The girl's father hated Ark, hated all

like him. The man reckoned he'd worked
hard enough to make his distance between

them and him, his family. When he found
out—and there is always a finding out—

he waited for the girl to come home from school,
cornered her in the entryway, slapped

her powerful hard across the mouth. By
instinct, the mother too slight recoiled,

but did not enter the mix. The metallic
taste of blood crept into the girl's mouth. She

walked silently to the bathroom, spit
a few times into the white porcelain

sink, did not answer the mother who so
quietly asked the girl if she was all

right, if she needed something. The girl felt
vacant. After that the girl laid low

a long while. In early winter she got
a late-shift clerk job at the hospital.

In the spring she graduated from
the high school, got a walk-up apartment

off a side street and down a small alley
in the little town across the wide, muddy river.

## Intermission

During this time Ark did not see the girl
often, sometimes at school, but not much. She

did not offer an explanation other
than to say she decided to get a job,

that she would explain later. Ark did not
know what she knew: that a cousin or

neighbor girl might see them together, might
let it slip at the wrong time in the wrong

place and then ... The nights grew cold and long.
In the spring she told him, but not enough.

# I Would Rather Go Blind

Ark and Lilith went on a year or so
like this: meeting late at night, sneaking as
though they were the ones who needed to feel
shame. It was a small town; she still fearful:
for herself, for Ark. Sometimes they would go
away, thirty or forty miles, to a park
upriver, a little restaurant in
another town. But sometimes is only
some times. The girl cried one night, sitting in
her yellow sundress on Ark's battered blue
couch, said she was sorry there couldn't be
more, something better. Some nights later Ark
rode to the hospital lot, just before
the end of her shift, to talk, to tell her
his idea, a plan. She was there, leaning
against some farm kid's pickup, sharing
a cigarette with him, twirling her hair.

# Ark Revs the Ghost Machine

Ark climbs the hill south of town walking first
under the viaduct, jumping over the creek,

edged with early winter ice, small and shallow
this time of year. He scrambles up the steep

incline then heads east, mid-ridge, parallel
to the creek, moving toward the center

of town. He can't see much, even in bright
day because the woods are heavy with white

oak, patches of yellow pine. Here and there
he catches glimpses: a spire, the high rise

that houses old folks. Some sounds rise, too: car
horns, men shouting, a backhoe backing up,

the noon whistle. He follows the ridge path
as it drops, meets the creek once again just

past the town line. He walks a railroad right
of way back, cuts behind the carpet mill,

catches Tenth Street, then Market. A few more
blocks and then goes into Old Sam's place.

Sam is serving two telephone workmen, but
turns, gives Ark a nod, says, *Ain't bad out t'day,*

*huh?* Ark shrugs, takes a stool seat at the short,
worn-Formica counter. *Won't kill you,* Ark

answers, motions his order in a shortcut
language understood by both men. Ark's pulse

comes down a bit, his breathing steadies, slows.
His engine still hums. He still thinks of her.

# Southbound

Tonight after sundown
I'm going to pack my case
I'll leave without a sound
Disappear without a trace

Ark went to the recruiting man. Then he
went away. Ark laid low. Mostly did what

he was told. Asked few questions. Didn't
really care. He blended in as best he

could. He shined his boots until they were
mirror bright. He ironed his shirts until

the creases were knife sharp. He went to places
he had not been. He did things he had not

done. When he could, he ran: one mile, two miles,
three, five. He focused on putting one foot

after another, looking ahead. And when he
could, he drank: two bottles, three bottles, five,

seven. And he tried hard to focus on
nothing at all, tried not looking back. He

got up every morning, made his bed, put
on his boots, went to breakfast. He did these

things over and over and over. Yet
even on the best days, it was not enough.

# Hearts of Stone

*And you cry because things get so strange so fast*
*And you cry because nothing good ever lasts*

There are few things worse than a crying drunk.
Ark had only been one once. It was a year

and a month later. He was in some dirt
bar in a harbor town somewhere south of

where he wanted to be. And he knew for
certain that now he was away. It was

his choice to escape, a choice that once made
was irreversible. Now in pity and

shame, Ark stares at the dank floor, a mix
of uneven wood and patches of busted

linoleum. He knows this kind of place
offers no type of sympathy, still he

wanders over to the unplugged jukebox
and reads the choices—an odd mix of country,

rock, and soul—pulls a token from his
pocket. Puts it back among some coins. Breathes

hard. Squares himself. Tomorrow, he thinks,
I'll still be away. I'll still be away.

# Ark Drives into the Night

A big rig is coming up fast. Its lights
go from far to closer to close. Barely
keeping it between the white lines, Ark welcomes
distraction. One hundred miles—maybe less—but
one hundred is a good number and when
more turns out to be less, then less is better,
a boost. State line sign, then gone. The big rig
that was riding his donkey faded off on
the hill climb. Lights in the distance: York.
Then Camp Hill. Might go east shore all the way
in daylight, but too many hills and curves, woods
and deer for nighttime. Instead Ark takes the low
river road with nothing much for sixty
miles, but porn shops, cheap motels, and truck stops.
Sixty miles, fifty-nine, fifty-eight.
Radio has country, preacher preaching, preaching,
country, pop, pop, preaching, pop, country. The moon
mirrors on the river, the water low
and flat as the road. Thirty-seven.
Thirty-four. A few more miles of darkness.

# Away

Ark walks tall and alert, head swiveling at regular intervals—left—then right—then left again. Next time the reverse. He walks all the way up the street, past the unused tracks at the east end of town, just before the hill, then back down the other side. Twice people wave to him. Twice he nods back, keeps moving.

It is too early. He does not think he can talk, not yet, but by now shops are either closing or putting on their lights. Ark turns sharp down Third Street, moves along the tracks for half a block, then pulls open the heavy wood door of Tony's Tavern. He walks to the far side of the empty u-shaped bar, sits down.

She comes out from the back-room kitchen, grabs a bottle from the cooler, uncaps it, and places it in front of Ark. Water beads on the cold bottle in the warm air. Ark grips it like a buoy in an open sea.

*Where the hell you been?* says she. *Away,* he replies, looks her up and down.

# Farther Down Up the Road

Ark's mind spins like a top. She stands there, asks
questions. Some he hears, and some he does not.
The whole time there's a red noise in his head
that churns in fast, irregular intervals like
an off-kilter carousel. *Ain't been back
much. Heard you have a kid now*, Ark says, looks
as close as he can to her. *Yeah, she's almost
two.* Ark makes a gesture, knocks over his now
half-empty beer bottle. Liquid puddles
on the scarred oak bar. She fetches
a rag, mops it up, tosses the bottle
in a bin. *New hands?* she asks. Ark smiles
a small smile. She starts to talk again, but
she looks away. In an involuntary single
motion she reaches into the cooler and
grabs another beer, sets it in front of Ark.
*You still like this kind?* she asks. *I switched,
but it'll do for now*, Ark says, swallows
the bile that's risen to the back of his throat.

# Play me a song I haven't heard before

Of course, you know how it works. Ark would wait
for her in his dark room on the nights she

could get away after her shift. She'd slip
from him as the sparrows sang in those

ephemeral moments right before
the first gray light of morning. Ark would rise too,

dress, head to work, maybe call her at lunch.
Some weeks they'd have an afternoon together.

Other weeks spared only a moment or two.
Ark wanted to leave. For them to leave. He'd

been other places. Knew other things. She needed
to stay, could only stay. She had not seen

other places, known of other ways. And
for her things had changed. Her mother,

courage found late but better than never,
moved into a new place with the girl

once she learned about the baby. Together
mother and daughter moved in a stilted

dance of acceptance, accommodation.
It worked well enough. The girl switched jobs,

tending bar evenings at Tony's Tavern
when the hospital went to outsourcing,

layoffs. Lilith stayed home days with her child.
Her mother worked part-time days, a cashier

at the new chain drug store, was the one put
the child to bed most nights. That winter was

a hard winter: early snow, bitter wind,
torpor-gray days. Ark trudged the town all

but the coldest nights. He kept to his
ways: alleys, shadows, now and then a few

blocks on Market, stopping in the little diner
to see Old Sam, have a coffee to ease

the chill. Sam knew Ark well, even before Ark
was a kid at the Sister's school. Knew more

than he supposed he should, more than he
let on. He knew Ark was troubled that winter,

but thought better than to ask. Ark was guarded,
discreet as a coydog in pasture grass

at wood's edge. Ark kept his own counsel, stood
full willing to bear whatever consequence.

# Crux

Ark knew what he did not want to know. Days
drifted into weeks. No calls. A call, then

an excuse. A few times Furman had Ark ride
along to auction, load and unload bikes.

Offered no counsel, just a beer when they
got back. Then came a call, a meeting, old

cliché, a talk. Home that night Ark felt like
busting something, but the few things that were

his were already damaged anyhow.
Ark wandered about town, jacket-less,

though it was chilly for nearly summer.
He walked up past the lot where the old

hotel once sat, taken down a few years
back, a precaution against gravity.

Looking east he saw the closed movie
house, some open stores, but empty ones, too.

He saw kids cruising past the park in farm
pickups and some in little imports with

spoilers and loud exhausts. He walked
neighborhoods he hadn't been in a while,

those with wider, tree-lined streets, fresh-painted
houses. He walked clear past the railroad bridge,

and the north bridge, and thought about crossing, but
didn't. She lived over there. He doubled

back, walked the tracks a while, crossed over
near the bowling alley, the housing project,

the shopping plaza that was new when he was
little, but faded now with broken signs and

second-rate stores. He was fast-walking and
sweating some by the time he made up his mind.

He had some blocks to go. When he got there,
Sam was alone in the place, bent behind

the counter, checking inventory, stocking up
for tomorrow. Ark placed a worn brass token

on the counter. "Good for one passage"
was written on it in small raised letters.

# Purgatory

Sam said he was fairly good when he was
younger: Did real well coming from country

folks surviving on a truck patch, chicken
house, and mill work. Somehow got to college,

became a lawyer. Did usual small town
stuff: wills, tenant contracts, tax forms. Nothing

to set the world on fire, but he was always
steady, a bachelor for years, until he

met her. Terrible, terrible thing what
happened. What they caused him. Tried killing

himself over it. Almost did. He was laid
up for months, never right after. His speech

wasn't right. His thinking clouded. He had some
good days, but he went hard to drink and that

didn't help. Went on for a while like that,
then one day he disappeared. Must have been

lost in the woods for a few days. Some thought
to drag the river but it was unusual

high that spring, dangerous. He come wandering
back into town, near ragged as a paper

birch. Even had a mongrel dog with him,
more likely as not a stray somebody

dumped in the country. Thought was a new
place since he was in a different part

of town and his memory no good. Some
thought it funny, but it wasn't, and most

just let it be. He took up with the woman
down there, and they were church-going folks, though

not married, because he still was, strictly
speaking. The woman helped him a lot, gave

him order and routine. Over the years
the novelty of the tragedy wore

out. Some forgot, some never knew. *In his
heart, I think he knew who you were,* Sam said.

*In his mind, not always.* Sam picked up
the token from the worn counter, raised it to

the light, his arm unsteady from palsy.
Sam's eyes held a glaze. He spoke again: *Not*

*many of us around still who ever used one
of these. Times change.* He handed the token

to Ark, who nestled it in his pocket,
where it felt somehow a bit heavier and

a bit lighter, somehow both at once.

# Rolling Hills and a Wide River

For how long Ark did not know. Maybe a month,
a year. What does it matter?                    There was him

and there was her. There was her who was not
complete with Ark. There was him who was not

Ark. Leaning against the cold river wall.
Walking narrow alleys. Home with stale

Chinese food at a table with a crooked
leg. It was all the same. Sometimes he had

hope, but it always punched him down, faded
like the sun sinking behind Blue Hill. He

thought her his best promise. He loved her voice.
The smell of her in the night. The feeling

of her hand in his. Gone now.          There was him
and there was her. Gone. Fair and unfair.

It was high summer. The sun was late
in the clouded sky. Ark stood on the bank

of the wide river, looked back at the green
hills rolling into the distance, then back

at the river. He stood there some minutes,
then spit into the swirling gray water.

# Survival Is Triumph Enough

Everyone knows that the south end of town
is lower. The neighborhood's streets share

dangerous drops off Front Street. Drivers not
wanting to belly scrape must baby crawl,

watch the angle going up or down
ever mindful of that incline. Across Front,

just past the pavement, a ten-foot wall runs
parallel to the river. Concrete near

a foot thick, built to hold back flood waters.
It did twice in years long past, some say it

won't hold again. You never know. If you
ask the right ones, a few might tell you

a story about Ark and the wall, how
Ark was running his cycle machine up and

down Walnut Street one night, gearing down near
the end, turning around and winding up

through the gears again, the engine sounding
higher, louder as he sped closer to Front.

Heard tell after one run, he simply braked,
made a left onto Front, then another onto

the bridge, the highway, then who knows. Some guy
said he saw him months later at a truck

stop up in the mountains a hundred miles
distant. Wouldn't let on who he was, left

quick. Another fellow said he was on
vacation down South, saw a guy walking

toward him on the street, spitting image.
The guy just nodded back, disappeared

into the crowd. Every so often some
jack who ain't got a spit of sense might

say he saw Ark in town, at the fair a few
years back or walking near the abandoned

tracks past East Chestnut. It's all a lie.
On that moon-bright night, Ark hit ninety,

one hundred, one hundred and ten miles
an hour, hit the end of Walnut, boomed up

that ramp, and just kept on going and going.
The moon was close high in the southern sky,

illuminating Clement Island and
the distant shore. And Ark was steady rising

until he disappeared. Doubt he's coming back.

# Epilogue:
# Enola Spelled Backward

You can't see the stars at night in Harrisburg
and Enola spelled backward is alone.

River fog hangs low on mid-September mornings
like this one. Year-round city lights and wooded

hills capped by Appalachian clouds conspire
to block the heavens. Over in Enola, the grandsons

of rail yard workers are fast-food shift managers
or drive forklifts hauling pallets stacked with sacks

of discount dog food from warehouse floor
to trailer truck dock. They don't travel down

to the freight yards wedged between the river
and the hill. There's little reason. Most of those jobs

are gone, ebbing like the springs and creeks
that fall into the river. If you listen right sometimes

you can still hear the high lonesome screech
of steel wheels on steel rails, the heavy, resonant

clank of cars coupling and uncoupling, shifting lines
and directions. We don't. Car windows rolled up tight,

we run the highways and east shore bypass, Williamsport
to York, going ten miles faster than the speed limit,

listening to jokes and songs from faraway places
on satellite radio, zipping past the hundred-year-old

Rockville Bridge: all those stones still holding their own
weight and more. Like the wide indifferent river

we ride beside, we never pay much mind to the signs
and towns we pass by. Sixty miles north, crews blast

through bedrock, building another bridge and bypass
past a town we'll soon never even know was there.

# Acknowledgments

The author is grateful to the Bloomsburg University Foundation and the Bloomsburg University College of Liberal Arts for awarding him the Jack and Helen Evans Endowed Faculty Fellowship, which provided time and resources to finish this collection. He is also grateful to the Chincoteague Bay Field Station in Chincoteague, Virginia, and The Porches Writing Retreat in Norwood, Virginia, for his residencies there.

He thanks the members of the "Second Monday Workshop Group" for their astute commentary: Shirl Boatman, Sarah Carro, Sarah Karasek, Richard Kahn, Bryne Lewis, and Matt Perakovich. Any deficiencies are the author's for not taking their advice.

Most of the poems in "Book I: Artemas," some in different versions, were published as a chapbook by Finishing Line Press. Much appreciation to them. The author is also grateful to the editors of the following publications in which some of these poems first appeared, some in different versions:

- *Fledging Rag*: "Happy as the day," "Moontown I," "Moontown III," and "Artemas on Good Friday."
- *Impost*: "Away" and "Hearts of Stone."
- *Listening to Water: The Susquehanna Watershed Anthology*: "Sunbury, Pa., 1957."
- *Modern Language Studies*: "The Yardmaster's Tower."
- *Word Fountain*: "Ark Drives into the Night."
- *Zingara Poetry Review*: "A Flower Rests" and "Night."

# Notes

• The opening quote from Frederick Douglass was encountered in David Blight's superlative 2018 biography, *Frederick Douglass: Prophet of Freedom*.

• Though there are references to Catholicism in this book, the second quote on the opening page is from the Revised English Version of the Bible, which can be found online. This version was chosen because of its use of language.

• In the poem "Artemas kills his woman," the words in italics are borrowed from "Dream Song #1" by John Berryman, from his major work *The Dreams Songs*, a narrative sequence containing 385 poems.

• The epigraph for the poem "Between Hell and Hell" is from the 1973 song "$1000 Wedding," written by Gram Parsons, an influential musician who is credited with being one of the creators of country rock. There are other echoes of the song in the poem. Parsons, who died at age 26, was reportedly kicked out of the Rolling Stones recording sessions for *Exile on Main Street* because his heavy drug and alcohol use was a bad influence on Keith Richards.

• The poem "There stand the glass" borrows its title from a country song that was a major hit for Webb Pierce in 1953. Both Pierce and Parsons had an affinity for Nudie suits, rhinestone-decorated suits made by Nudie Cohn. Pierce had a "There Stands the Glass" suit with a stylized cocktail spilling out over the back of the jacket. Parsons wears a Nudie suit emblazoned with marijuana leaves and barbiturate pills on the cover the of 1969 Flying Burrito Brothers album *The Gilded Palace of Sin*.

• The poem "Artemas Lives" contains the Latin phrase *In nomine patris et filii et spiritus* sancti. It means "in the name of the Father, and the Son, and the Holy Spirit." Masses in the Catholic Church were conducted in Latin until 1965.

• The epigraph of the poem "Farmer" is from the song "I Shot the Sheriff" written by Bob Marley and appears on the 1973 album *Burnin'* by The Wailers. The soft-rock version recorded by Eric Clapton is an abomination.

• The title of the poem "I Would Rather Go Blind" was taken from a song of the same name recorded by Etta James in 1967. It is considered a Soul music classic. Who, exactly, wrote the song is unclear, with James claiming the gist of the song was given to her by a friend, Ellington Jordan, when she visited him in prison. It is co-credited to Jordan, James, and singer Billy Foster. It has been covered by many others including B.B. King and Rod Stewart.

• The title of the poem "Southbound" is taken from a 1977 Thin Lizzy song of the same name. The epigraph is from the song.

• The title of the poem "Hearts of Stone" is taken by a song of the same name written by Bruce Springsteen. It was recorded by Southside Johnny and the Ashbury Jukes on their 1978 album of the same name is arguably their most popular song. The epigraph is from the song.

• The title of the poem "Farther Down Up the Road" is a variation on lyrics found in the Blues standard "Farther Up the Road" first recorded by Bobby "Blue" Bland in 1957. Some may know Clapton's versions. Listen to the original.

• The title of the poem "Survival Is Triumph Enough" is a quote attributed to the writer Harry Crews. It is also the title of a 2007 documentary film about him.

• Kacie England, then a student at Bloomsburg University, spoke the opening line of "Enola Spelled Backward" in class one day. It is borrowed, with permission, from her.

• Completed in 1902, the Rockville Bridge is older than the one hundred years attributed to it in "Enola Spelled Backward." The bridge is located about five miles north of Harrisburg, Pennsylvania, and is on the National Register of Historic Places.

Other poetry collections by **Jerry Wemple** include *You Can See It from Here,* which won the Naomi Long Madgett Poetry Award, and *The Civil War in Baltimore,* as well as two chapbooks. He is co-editor, along with Marjorie Maddox, of the anthology *Common Wealth: Contemporary Poets on Pennsylvania.* His poems and creative nonfiction have been published in numerous anthologies and journals, including internationally in Ireland, Chile, and Canada. He has received several awards for his teaching and writing including a Fellowship in Literature from the Pennsylvania Council on the Arts, The *Word Journal* Chapbook Prize, and the Jack and Helen Evans Endowed Faculty Fellowship from the Bloomsburg University Foundation. He teaches at Bloomsburg University of Pennsylvania. For more information, visit his website www.jwemple.com.

CPSIA information can be obtained
at www.ICGtesting.com
Printed in the USA
BVHW032331051020
590351BV00001B/34